Spotter's Guide to
TREES

Esmond Harris
Director of the Royal Forestry Society

Illustrated by
Annabel Milne & Peter Stebbing

Puffin Books

Contents

Designed by
Sally Burrough

Edited by
Ingrid Selberg and
Sue Jacquemier

Additional illustrations by
Christine Howes

First published in 1978 by
Usborne Publishing Limited,
20 Garrick Street, London WC2
Published in Puffin Books 1978

Text and Artwork © 1978 by
Usborne Publishing Limited

Printed by
Mateu Cromo Artes Graficas, S.A.
Madrid, Spain.

Acknowledgements
The illustrators would like to acknowledge the
help of the staff of the Royal Botanical Gardens
at Kew, with special thanks to Ruth Messom.
They also thank Dr Martin Rix at the Royal
Horticultural Society Gardens at Wisley, and
Peter Orriss of the Cambridge University
Botanical Gardens.

How to Use this Book

This book is an identification guide to some of the trees of Britain and Europe. Take it with you when you go out spotting. Not all of these trees will be common in your area, but many may be found in large gardens or parks. (See page 60 for a list of places to visit.)

The book is arranged with conifers first, followed by broad-leaved trees and shrubs. Trees that are closely related, for example all the Oaks, are grouped together.

The illustrations show important features that will help you to identify a tree at any time of the year. For each type of tree, the leaf, the bark, the shape of a full-grown tree in full leaf and its shape in winter (if the tree is deciduous) are always shown. Flowers and fruits (including cones) are also illustrated if they will help you to identify the tree.

The description next to each illustration gives you additional information to help you identify trees. The average height of a full-grown tree is written next to each illustration.

Remember that there are many clues to help you recognize a tree, not just the leaves, so look carefully at the bark, the tree's shape and other features.

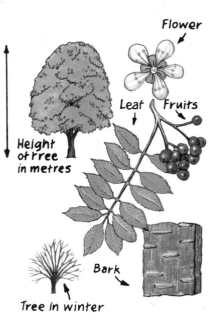

Flower

Leaf   Fruits

Height of tree in metres

Bark

Tree in winter

Beside the description is a small blank circle. Each time you spot a new tree, make a tick in the circle.

Scorecard

At the back of the book is a score-card which gives you a score for each tree you spot. A common tree scores 5 points, and a very rare one is worth 25 points. If you like, you can add up your score after a day out spotting.

Page	Tree	Score	Date Mar 2	Date Mar 10	Date Apr 3
6	Scots Pine	5	5	5	5
6	Maritime Pine	15		15	
7	Stone Pine	25			

Parts of a Tree

A tree is a plant that grows on a single, central woody stem. A shrub is usually smaller and has many stems.

Trees are divided into two main groups: **conifers** and **broadleaved trees.** Most broadleaved trees have broad flat leaves (which they drop in winter) and they have seeds which are enclosed in fruits (nuts or other forms). Most conifers have narrow, needle-like or scaly leaves. Their fruits are usually woody cones.

Most broadleaved trees are **deciduous** which means that they lose their leaves in the autumn and grow new ones again in the spring. Most conifers are **evergreen,** meaning that they keep their green leaves throughout the winter.

These pictures show the different parts of a tree and explain some of the words that appear in the book.

Leaves

There are many different shapes of leaves. Some of the most common ones are shown here.
A leaf that is in one piece is called **simple.**

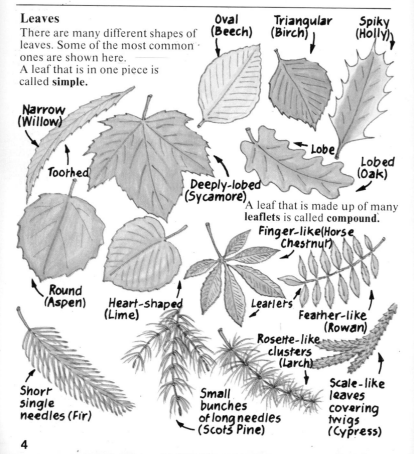

Oval (Beech)

Triangular (Birch)

Spiky (Holly)

Narrow (Willow)

Lobe

Lobed (Oak)

Toothed

Deeply-lobed (Sycamore)

A leaf that is made up of many **leaflets** is called **compound.**

Finger-like (Horse Chestnut)

Round (Aspen)

Heart-shaped (Lime)

Leaflets

Feather-like (Rowan)

Rosette-like clusters (Larch)

Short single needles (Fir)

Small bunches of long needles (Scots Pine)

Scale-like leaves covering twigs (Cypress)

Flowers

All trees have flowers that develop into fruits. Here are some different types of flowers.

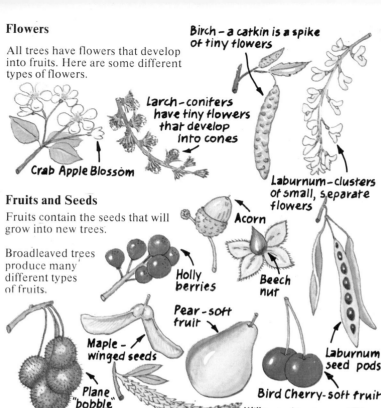

Birch – a catkin is a spike of tiny flowers

Larch – conifers have tiny flowers that develop into cones

Crab Apple Blossom

Laburnum – clusters of small, separate flowers

Fruits and Seeds

Fruits contain the seeds that will grow into new trees.

Broadleaved trees produce many different types of fruits.

Holly berries

Acorn

Beech nut

Pear – soft fruit

Maple – winged seeds

Plane "bobble"

Laburnum seed pods

Bird Cherry – soft fruit

Willow – downy seeds

cone scale

seed

Bract

seed

scale

bract

A cone is the woody fruit of a conifer and is made up of many overlapping scales bearing seeds. Cones come in many different shapes and sizes.

A **bract** is a leaf-like structure at the base of a cone scale. Only some cones have bracts that show.

Bark is the hard protective outer covering of the trunk. It can be furrowed or smooth.

The **crown** of a tree is its leafy top. Crown shapes vary a lot.

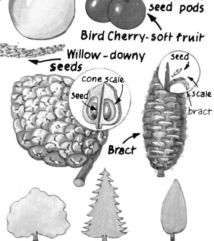

Broad (Oak)

Cone-shaped (Norway Spruce)

Narrow (Lombardy Poplar)

Conifers

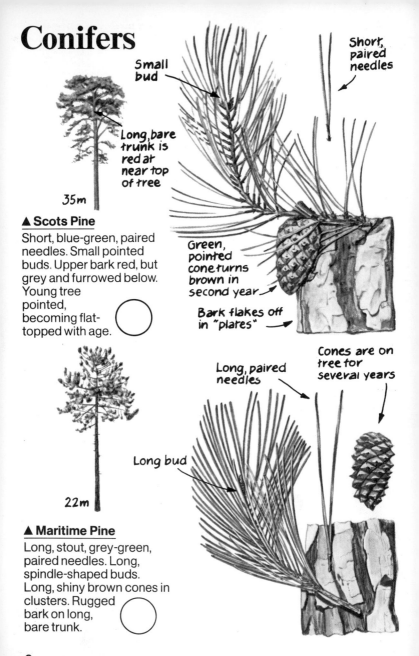

Small bud

Short, paired needles

Long, bare trunk is red at near top of tree

35m

▲ Scots Pine

Short, blue-green, paired needles. Small pointed buds. Upper bark red, but grey and furrowed below. Young tree pointed, becoming flat-topped with age.

Green, pointed cone turns brown in second year

Bark flakes off in "plates"

Cones are on tree for several years

Long, paired needles

Long bud

22m

▲ Maritime Pine

Long, stout, grey-green, paired needles. Long, spindle-shaped buds. Long, shiny brown cones in clusters. Rugged bark on long, bare trunk.

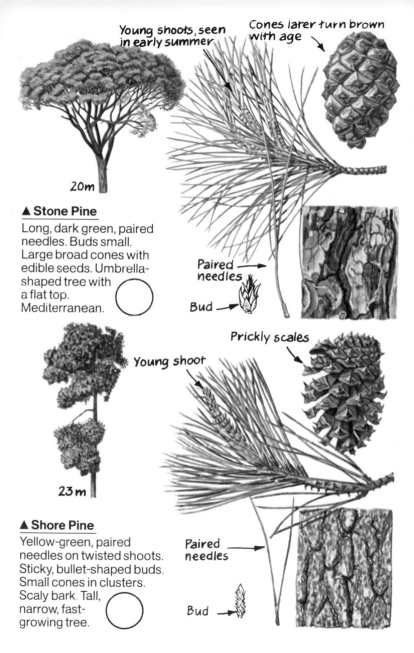

Young shoots, seen in early summer

Cones later turn brown with age

▲ Stone Pine

Long, dark green, paired needles. Buds small. Large broad cones with edible seeds. Umbrella-shaped tree with a flat top. Mediterranean.

20m

Paired needles

Bud

Prickly scales

Young shoot

▲ Shore Pine

Yellow-green, paired needles on twisted shoots. Sticky, bullet-shaped buds. Small cones in clusters. Scaly bark. Tall, narrow, fast-growing tree.

23m

Paired needles

Bud

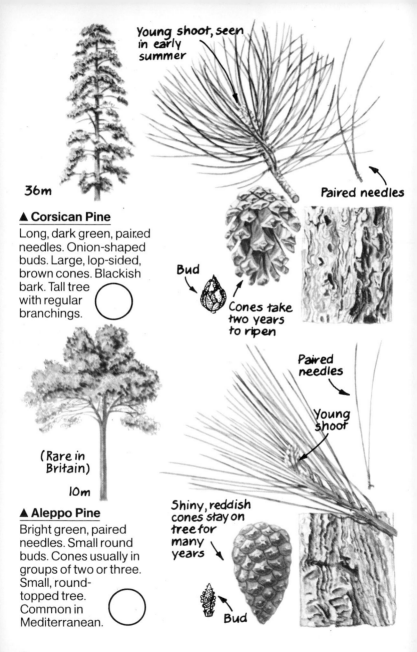

Young shoot, seen in early summer

Paired needles

36m

▲ Corsican Pine

Long, dark green, paired needles. Onion-shaped buds. Large, lop-sided, brown cones. Blackish bark. Tall tree with regular branchings.

Bud

Cones take two years to ripen

Paired needles

Young shoot

(Rare in Britain)

10m

▲ Aleppo Pine

Bright green, paired needles. Small round buds. Cones usually in groups of two or three. Small, round-topped tree. Common in Mediterranean.

Shiny, reddish cones stay on tree for many years

Bud

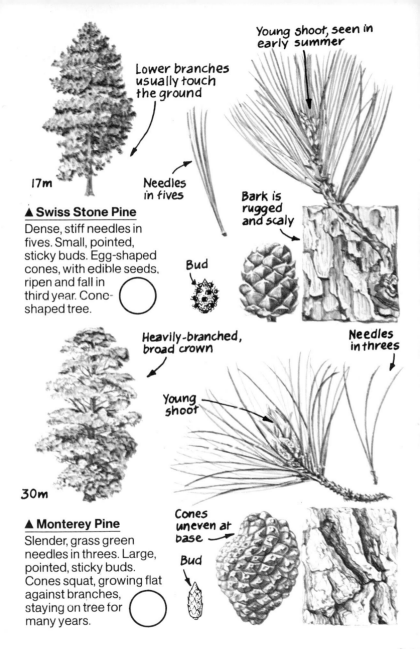

Young shoot, seen in early summer

Lower branches usually touch the ground

17m

Needles in fives

Bark is rugged and scaly

▲ Swiss Stone Pine

Dense, stiff needles in fives. Small, pointed, sticky buds. Egg-shaped cones, with edible seeds, ripen and fall in third year. Cone-shaped tree.

Bud

Heavily-branched, broad crown

Needles in threes

Young shoot

30m

Cones uneven at base

Bud

▲ Monterey Pine

Slender, grass green needles in threes. Large, pointed, sticky buds. Cones squat, growing flat against branches, staying on tree for many years.

9

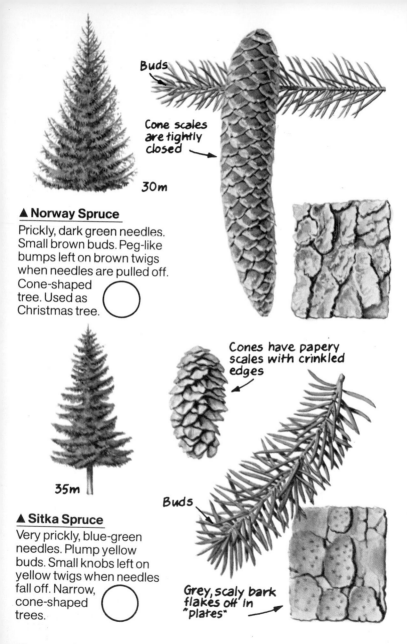

Buds

Cone scales
are tightly
closed

30m

▲ Norway Spruce

Prickly, dark green needles.
Small brown buds. Peg-like
bumps left on brown twigs
when needles are pulled off.
Cone-shaped
tree. Used as
Christmas tree.

Cones have papery
scales with crinkled
edges

35m

Buds

▲ Sitka Spruce

Very prickly, blue-green
needles. Plump yellow
buds. Small knobs left on
yellow twigs when needles
fall off. Narrow,
cone-shaped
trees.

Grey, scaly bark
flakes off in
"plates"

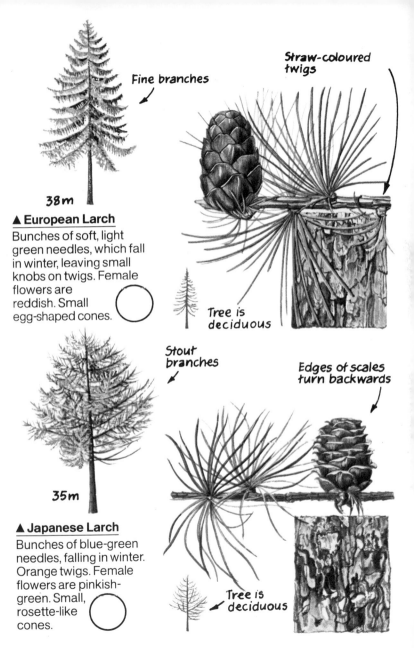

Fine branches

Straw-coloured twigs

38m

▲ European Larch

Bunches of soft, light green needles, which fall in winter, leaving small knobs on twigs. Female flowers are reddish. Small egg-shaped cones.

Tree is deciduous

Stout branches

Edges of scales turn backwards

35m

▲ Japanese Larch

Bunches of blue-green needles, falling in winter. Orange twigs. Female flowers are pinkish-green. Small, rosette-like cones.

Tree is deciduous

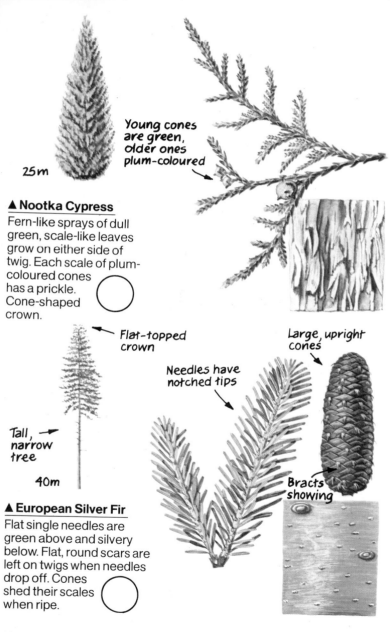

Young cones
are green,
older ones
plum-coloured

25 m

▲ Nootka Cypress

Fern-like sprays of dull
green, scale-like leaves
grow on either side of
twig. Each scale of plum-
coloured cones
has a prickle.
Cone-shaped
crown.

Flat-topped
crown

Needles have
notched tips

Large, upright
cones

Tall,
narrow
tree

40 m

Bracts
showing

▲ European Silver Fir

Flat single needles are
green above and silvery
below. Flat, round scars are
left on twigs when needles
drop off. Cones
shed their scales
when ripe.

30m

▲ Greek Fir

Shiny green, spiny-tipped needles all round twig. Tall, narrow cones shed scales to leave bare spike on tree. Common in parks.

Pointed tip

Bark flakes off in "plates" ➞

28m

▲ Spanish Fir

Short, blunt, blue-grey needles all round twig. Cylindrical, upright cones fall apart on tree. Found only in gardens in Britain.

Blunt tip

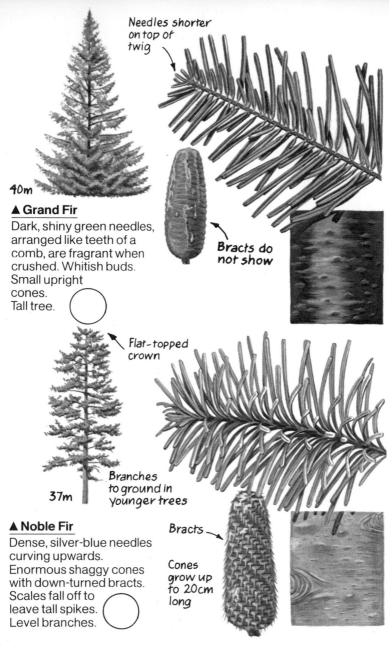

Needles shorter on top of twig

40m

▲ Grand Fir

Dark, shiny green needles, arranged like teeth of a comb, are fragrant when crushed. Whitish buds. Small upright cones. Tall tree.

Bracts do not show

Flat-topped crown

Branches to ground in younger trees

37m

▲ Noble Fir

Dense, silver-blue needles curving upwards. Enormous shaggy cones with down-turned bracts. Scales fall off to leave tall spikes. Level branches.

Bracts

Cones grow up to 20cm long

14

Beech-like bud

Needles are parted on twig

Bracts

▲ Douglas Fir
Soft fragrant needles.
Long-pointed, copper-brown buds. Light brown, hanging cones with three-pointed bracts.
Old bark is thick and corky.

Leader droops

Young cones are green, older ones are brown

Cone has a few rounded scales

Tips of branches droop

Flattened needles

40m

35m

▲ Western Hemlock
Needles various lengths, green above and silver below. Small cones on shoot tips. Smooth, brown scaly bark.
Branch tips and top shoot droops.

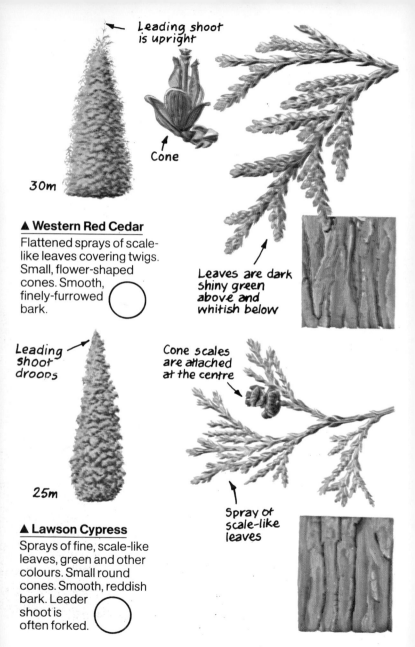

Leading shoot
is upright

Cone

30m

▲ Western Red Cedar
Flattened sprays of scale-like leaves covering twigs. Small, flower-shaped cones. Smooth, finely-furrowed bark.

Leaves are dark shiny green above and whitish below

Leading shoot droops

Cone scales are attached at the centre

25m

▲ Lawson Cypress
Sprays of fine, scale-like leaves, green and other colours. Small round cones. Smooth, reddish bark. Leader shoot is often forked.

Spray of scale-like leaves

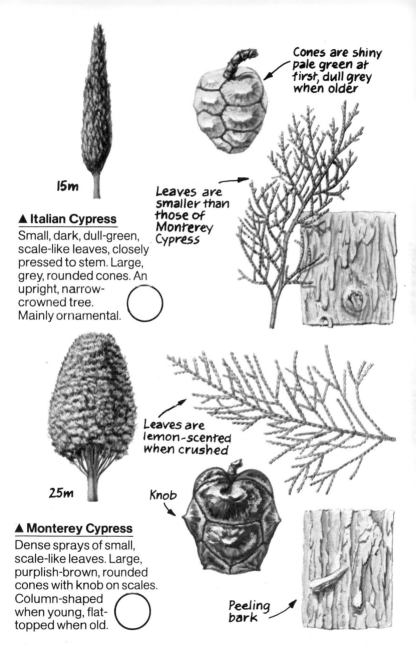

Cones are shiny pale green at first, dull grey when older

15m

Leaves are smaller than those of Monterey Cypress

▲ Italian Cypress

Small, dark, dull-green, scale-like leaves, closely pressed to stem. Large, grey, rounded cones. An upright, narrow-crowned tree. Mainly ornamental.

25m

Leaves are lemon-scented when crushed

Knob

▲ Monterey Cypress

Dense sprays of small, scale-like leaves. Large, purplish-brown, rounded cones with knob on scales. Column-shaped when young, flat-topped when old.

Peeling bark

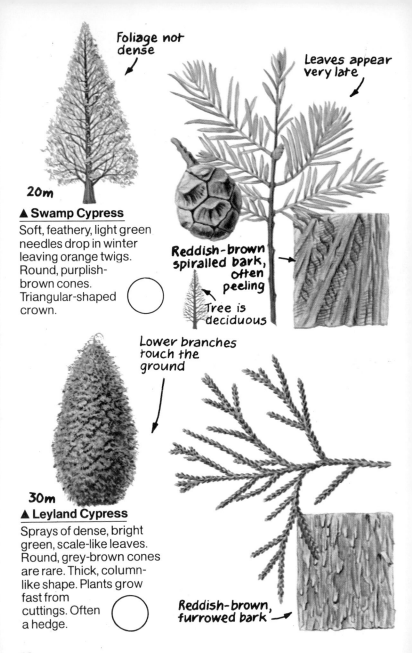

Foliage not dense

Leaves appear very late

20m

▲ Swamp Cypress

Soft, feathery, light green needles drop in winter leaving orange twigs. Round, purplish-brown cones. Triangular-shaped crown.

Reddish-brown spiralled bark, often peeling

Tree is deciduous

Lower branches touch the ground

30m

▲ Leyland Cypress

Sprays of dense, bright green, scale-like leaves. Round, grey-brown cones are rare. Thick, column-like shape. Plants grow fast from cuttings. Often a hedge.

Reddish-brown, furrowed bark

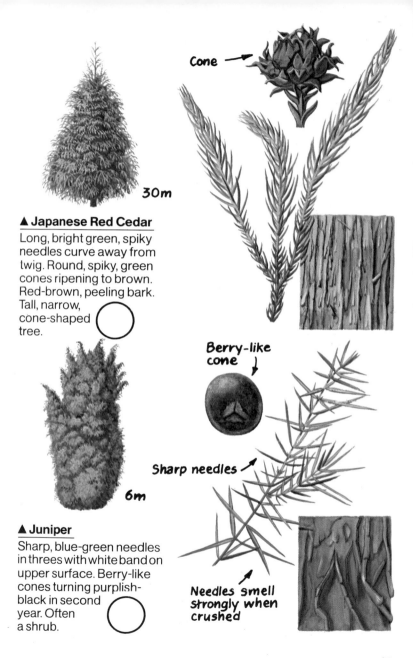

Cone

▲ Japanese Red Cedar

Long, bright green, spiky
needles curve away from
twig. Round, spiky, green
cones ripening to brown.
Red-brown, peeling bark.
Tall, narrow,
cone-shaped
tree.

30m

Berry-like
cone

Sharp needles

▲ Juniper

Sharp, blue-green needles
in threes with white band on
upper surface. Berry-like
cones turning purplish-
black in second
year. Often
a shrub.

6m

Needles smell
strongly when
crushed

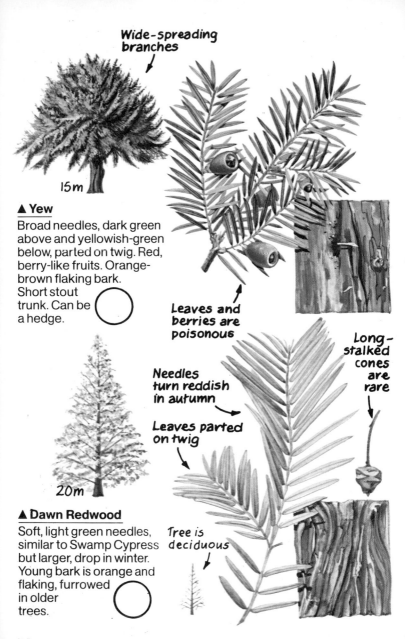

Wide-spreading branches

▲ Yew
Broad needles, dark green above and yellowish-green below, parted on twig. Red, berry-like fruits. Orange-brown flaking bark. Short stout trunk. Can be a hedge.

15m

Leaves and berries are poisonous

Needles turn reddish in autumn

Leaves parted on twig

Long-stalked cones are rare

▲ Dawn Redwood
Soft, light green needles, similar to Swamp Cypress but larger, drop in winter. Young bark is orange and flaking, furrowed in older trees.

20m

Tree is deciduous

33m

Needles parted on either side of twig →

▲ Coast Redwood

Hard, sharp-pointed needles, dark green above and white-banded below. Small, round cones. Thick, reddish, spongy bark. Tall tree.

38m

Foliage hanging from upswept branches ↙

Diamond-shaped cone scales wrinkle when they ripen ↙

▲ Wellingtonia

Deep green, scale-like, pointed leaves. Long-stalked, round, corky cones. Soft, thick, deeply-furrowed bark. Tall tree with upswept branches.

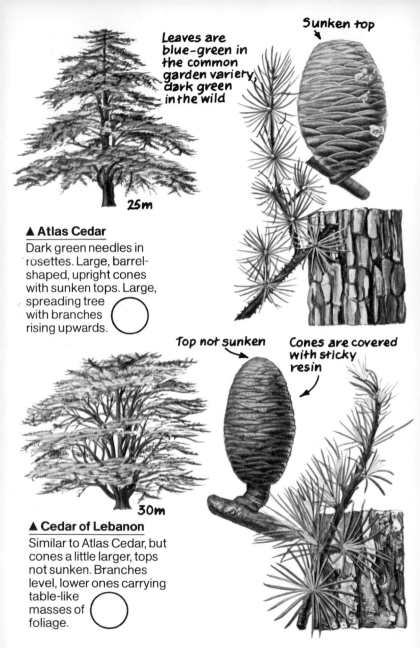

Leaves are blue-green in the common garden variety, dark green in the wild

Sunken top

▲ Atlas Cedar

Dark green needles in rosettes. Large, barrel-shaped, upright cones with sunken tops. Large, spreading tree with branches rising upwards.

25m

Top not sunken

Cones are covered with sticky resin

▲ Cedar of Lebanon

Similar to Atlas Cedar, but cones a little larger, tops not sunken. Branches level, lower ones carrying table-like masses of foliage.

30m

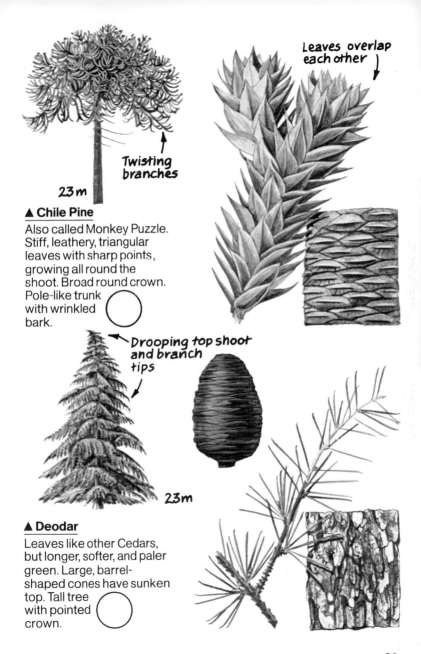

Leaves overlap each other

Twisting branches

23 m

▲ Chile Pine

Also called Monkey Puzzle. Stiff, leathery, triangular leaves with sharp points, growing all round the shoot. Broad round crown. Pole-like trunk with wrinkled bark.

Drooping top shoot and branch tips

23m

▲ Deodar

Leaves like other Cedars, but longer, softer, and paler green. Large, barrel-shaped cones have sunken top. Tall tree with pointed crown.

Broadleaved Trees

Long-stalked, tall acorn

Acorn cup

Lobe

Long stalk

▲ **English Oak**

Leaves short-stalked with ear-like lobes at base. Broad crown. Trunk shorter than Sessile Oak. Many large branches growing from same point.

23m

All veins go to tips of lobes

Acorn more rounded than on Common Oak

21m

▲ **Sessile Oak**

Thick, dark green, long-stalked leaves tapering to base. Branches grow from stem at different levels and point upwards in narrow crown.

Often stalkless

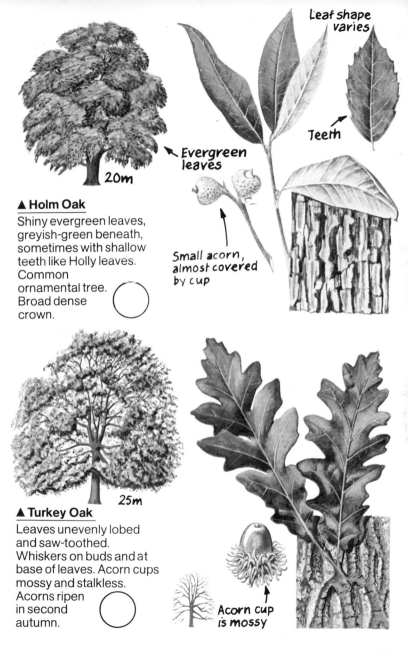

Leaf shape varies

Teeth

Evergreen leaves

▲ Holm Oak

Shiny evergreen leaves, greyish-green beneath, sometimes with shallow teeth like Holly leaves. Common ornamental tree. Broad dense crown.

20m

Small acorn, almost covered by cup

▲ Turkey Oak

Leaves unevenly lobed and saw-toothed. Whiskers on buds and at base of leaves. Acorn cups mossy and stalkless. Acorns ripen in second autumn.

25m

Acorn cup is mossy

16m

▲ Cork Oak

Shiny evergreen leaves with wavy edge. Thick, corky, whitish bark. Small tree, except in warmer countries.
Common in southern Europe.

Twisted trunk and branches

Acorn

Cork is obtained from the bark

Autumn colour of leaves

20m

▲ Red Oak

Large leaves with bristly-tipped lobes, turn reddish-brown in autumn. Squat acorns in shallow cups ripen in second year. Smooth silvery bark.

Acorn

25m

▲ Common Ash

Compound leaf of 9-13 leaflets appearing late, after bunches of purplish flowers. Clusters of "keys" stay on the tree into winter. Pale grey bark.

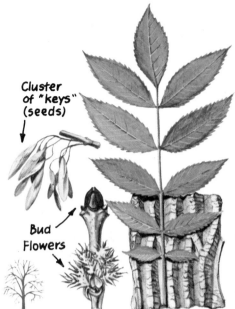

Cluster of "keys" (seeds)

Bud

Flowers

20m

▲ Manna Ash

Compound leaf of 5-9 stalked leaflets. Clusters of showy white flowers in May. Smooth grey bark oozes sugary liquid called manna.

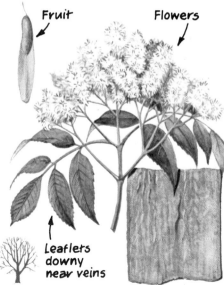

Fruit

Flowers

Leaflets downy near veins

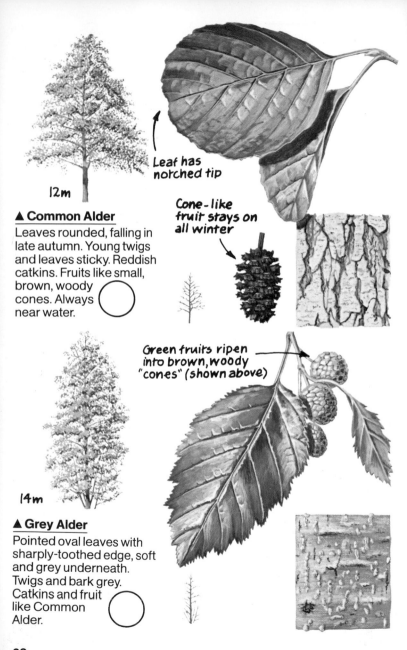

12m

▲ Common Alder

Leaves rounded, falling in late autumn. Young twigs and leaves sticky. Reddish catkins. Fruits like small, brown, woody cones. Always near water.

Leaf has notched tip

Cone-like fruit stays on all winter

14m

▲ Grey Alder

Pointed oval leaves with sharply-toothed edge, soft and grey underneath. Twigs and bark grey. Catkins and fruit like Common Alder.

Green fruits ripen into brown, woody "cones" (shown above)

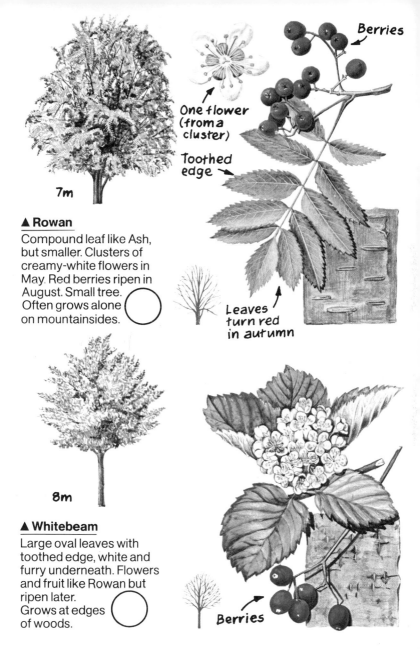

Berries

One flower (from a cluster)

Toothed edge

7m

Leaves turn red in autumn

▲ Rowan

Compound leaf like Ash, but smaller. Clusters of creamy-white flowers in May. Red berries ripen in August. Small tree. Often grows alone on mountainsides.

8m

▲ Whitebeam

Large oval leaves with toothed edge, white and furry underneath. Flowers and fruit like Rowan but ripen later. Grows at edges of woods.

Berries

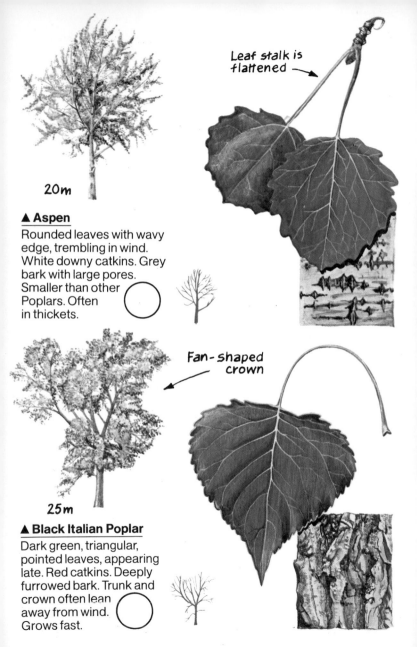

Leaf stalk is flattened →

20 m

▲ Aspen
Rounded leaves with wavy edge, trembling in wind. White downy catkins. Grey bark with large pores. Smaller than other Poplars. Often in thickets.

Fan-shaped crown

25 m

▲ Black Italian Poplar
Dark green, triangular, pointed leaves, appearing late. Red catkins. Deeply furrowed bark. Trunk and crown often lean away from wind. Grows fast.

30

20m

▲ White Poplar

Five-lobed leaves are
downy white underneath.
Entire crown looks white.
Lower bark dark and
rugged, upper
bark pale grey.
Crown often
leaning.

Wavy
edges

Under-
side of
leaf

Lower
leaves are
less lobed

Diamond-shaped marks
on young bark

Large, fast-
growing tree

35m

▲ Western Balsam Poplar

Large, triangular, pointed
leaves, white underneath.
Buds and young leaves
sticky and sweet-smelling.
Long purplish
catkins. White
fluffy seeds.

Underside
of leaf

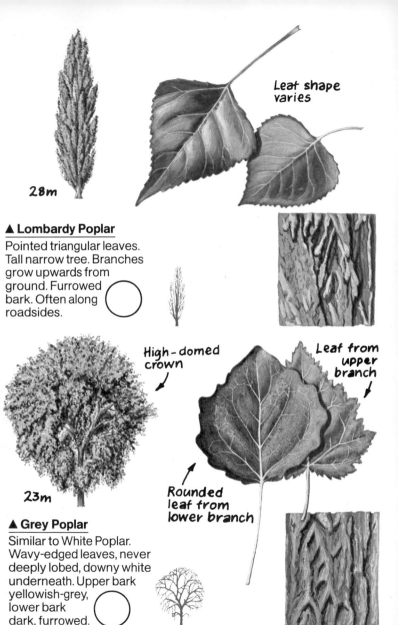

Leaf shape varies

28m

▲ Lombardy Poplar
Pointed triangular leaves.
Tall narrow tree. Branches
grow upwards from
ground. Furrowed
bark. Often along
roadsides.

High-domed crown

Leaf from upper branch

Rounded leaf from lower branch

23m

▲ Grey Poplar
Similar to White Poplar.
Wavy-edged leaves, never
deeply lobed, downy white
underneath. Upper bark
yellowish-grey,
lower bark
dark, furrowed.

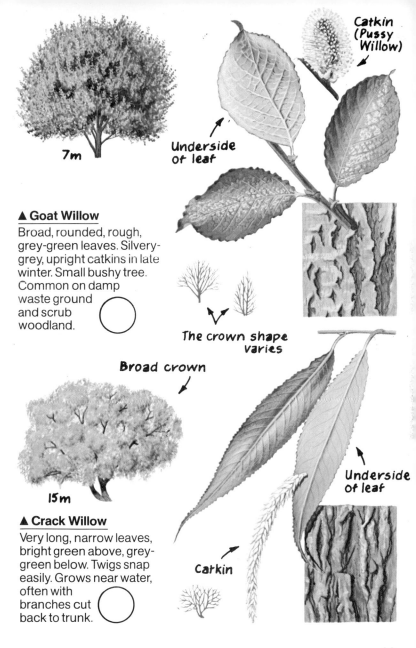

7m

Catkin (Pussy Willow)

Underside of leaf

The crown shape varies

▲ Goat Willow
Broad, rounded, rough, grey-green leaves. Silvery-grey, upright catkins in late winter. Small bushy tree. Common on damp waste ground and scrub woodland.

Broad crown

15m

Underside of leaf

Catkin

▲ Crack Willow
Very long, narrow leaves, bright green above, grey-green below. Twigs snap easily. Grows near water, often with branches cut back to trunk.

20m

▲ White Willow

Long, narrow, finely-toothed leaves, white underneath. Slender twigs, hard to break. Common by water. Weeping Willow is a variety with trailing branches.

Underside of leaf

Catkin

15m

▲ Silver Birch

Small, diamond-shaped leaves with double-toothed edge. Long "lamb's tail" catkins in April. Slender tree with drooping branches.

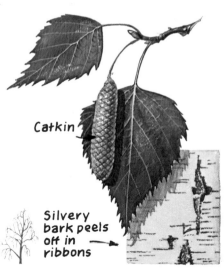

Catkin

Silvery bark peels off in ribbons

34

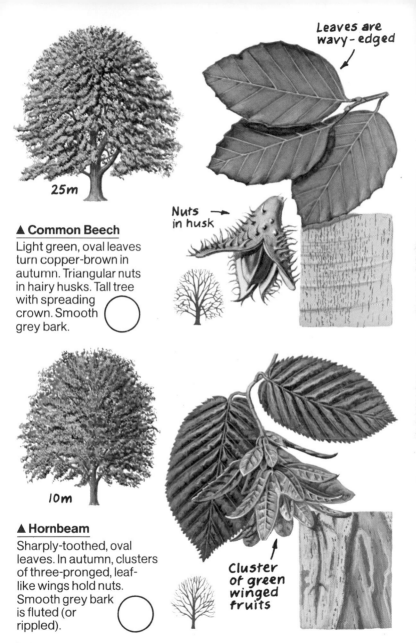

Leaves are
wavy-edged

25m

Nuts
in husk

▲ Common Beech

Light green, oval leaves
turn copper-brown in
autumn. Triangular nuts
in hairy husks. Tall tree
with spreading
crown. Smooth
grey bark.

10m

▲ Hornbeam

Sharply-toothed, oval
leaves. In autumn, clusters
of three-pronged, leaf-
like wings hold nuts.
Smooth grey bark
is fluted (or
rippled).

Cluster
of green
winged
fruits

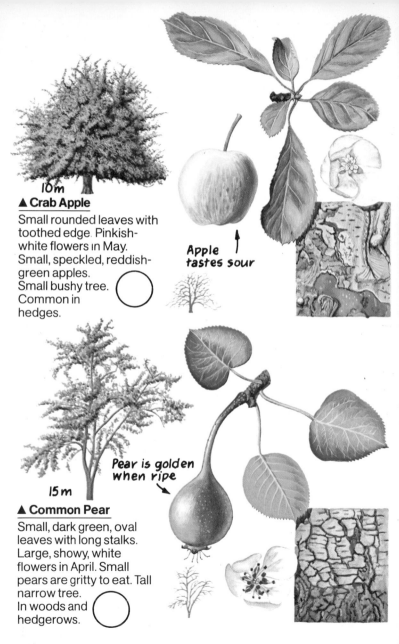

10m

▲ Crab Apple

Small rounded leaves with toothed edge. Pinkish-white flowers in May. Small, speckled, reddish-green apples. Small bushy tree. Common in hedges.

Apple tastes sour

Pear is golden when ripe

15m

▲ Common Pear

Small, dark green, oval leaves with long stalks. Large, showy, white flowers in April. Small pears are gritty to eat. Tall narrow tree. In woods and hedgerows.

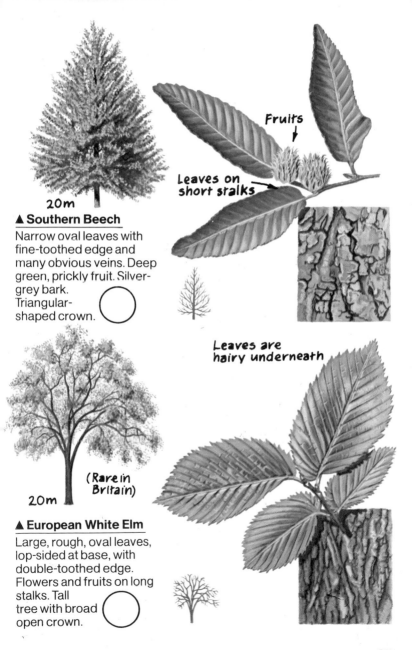

▲ Southern Beech

Narrow oval leaves with fine-toothed edge and many obvious veins. Deep green, prickly fruit. Silver-grey bark. Triangular-shaped crown.

20m

Fruits

Leaves on short stalks

Leaves are hairy underneath

▲ European White Elm

Large, rough, oval leaves, lop-sided at base, with double-toothed edge. Flowers and fruits on long stalks. Tall tree with broad open crown.

20m

(Rare in Britain)

37

30m

▲ London Plane

Large broad leaves with pointed lobes. Spiny "bobble" fruits hanging all winter. Flaking bark leaving yellowish patches. Tall tree, often in towns.

Fruit

20m

▲ Sycamore

Dark green, leathery leaves with five lobes. Paired, closely-angled, winged seeds. Large spreading tree. Smooth brown bark becoming scaly.

Toothed edge

Seeds twist as they fall

Leaves turn golden in autumn

▲ Norway Maple

Light green, thin leaves. Lobes and teeth are bristle-tipped. Paired seeds form wide angle. Smaller, less spreading than Sycamore. Finely-furrowed, grey bark.

15m

Pairs of seeds spin as they fall

Lobes are blunt

Leaves turn golden in autumn

▲ Field Maple

Small, dark green leaves with five lobes. Small, reddish, winged seeds form a straight line. Small tree with round head. Often in hedges.

10m

Seeds

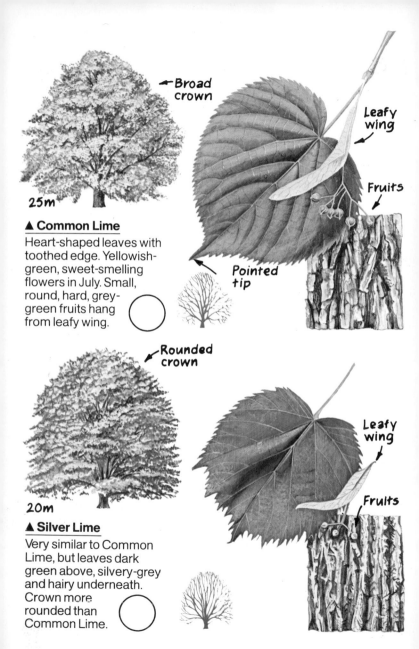

Broad crown

25m

Leafy wing

Fruits

Pointed tip

▲ Common Lime

Heart-shaped leaves with toothed edge. Yellowish-green, sweet-smelling flowers in July. Small, round, hard, grey-green fruits hang from leafy wing.

Rounded crown

20m

Leafy wing

Fruits

▲ Silver Lime

Very similar to Common Lime, but leaves dark green above, silvery-grey and hairy underneath. Crown more rounded than Common Lime.

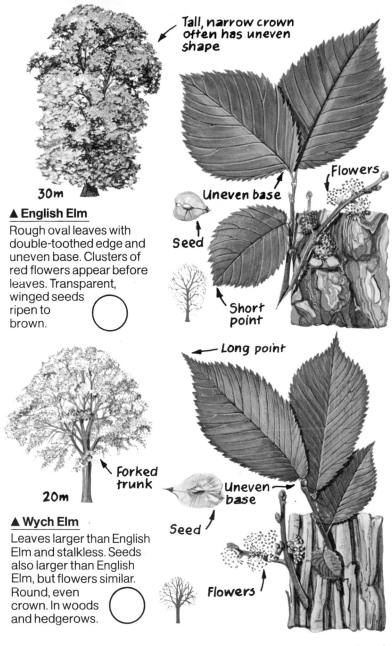

Tall, narrow crown often has uneven shape

Flowers

Uneven base

Seed

Short point

30m

▲ English Elm

Rough oval leaves with double-toothed edge and uneven base. Clusters of red flowers appear before leaves. Transparent, winged seeds ripen to brown.

Long point

Uneven base

Seed

Flowers

20m

Forked trunk

▲ Wych Elm

Leaves larger than English Elm and stalkless. Seeds also larger than English Elm, but flowers similar. Round, even crown. In woods and hedgerows.

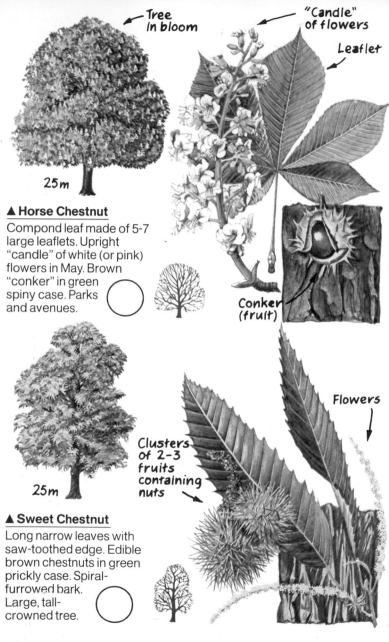

Tree in bloom

"Candle" of flowers

Leaflet

25m

▲ Horse Chestnut

Compond leaf made of 5-7 large leaflets. Upright "candle" of white (or pink) flowers in May. Brown "conker" in green spiny case. Parks and avenues.

Conker (fruit)

Flowers

Clusters of 2-3 fruits containing nuts

25m

▲ Sweet Chestnut

Long narrow leaves with saw-toothed edge. Edible brown chestnuts in green prickly case. Spiral-furrowed bark. Large, tall-crowned tree.

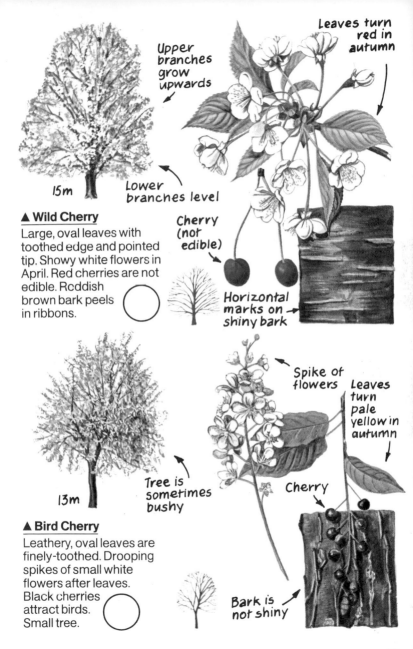

Upper branches grow upwards

Leaves turn red in autumn

Lower branches level

15m

▲ Wild Cherry

Large, oval leaves with toothed edge and pointed tip. Showy white flowers in April. Red cherries are not edible. Reddish brown bark peels in ribbons.

Cherry (not edible)

Horizontal marks on shiny bark

Spike of flowers

Leaves turn pale yellow in autumn

Cherry

Tree is sometimes bushy

13m

▲ Bird Cherry

Leathery, oval leaves are finely-toothed. Drooping spikes of small white flowers after leaves. Black cherries attract birds. Small tree.

Bark is not shiny

Unripe fruit

Ripe fruit

Young fruits

Old trees have branches to the ground and often lean over

▲ Black Mulberry

Rough, heart-shaped leaves with toothed edge. Short catkins. Edible, blackish-red berries. Low, broad-crowned tree. Short trunk and twisted branches.

12m

Smooth, green case containing edible walnut

Young fruit

▲ Common Walnut

Compound leaves of 7-9 untoothed leaflets. Twigs are hollow, with cross-sections inside. Smooth grey bark with some cracks, or fissures. Broad crown.

15m

Leaves are bronze when they first open, turning green later

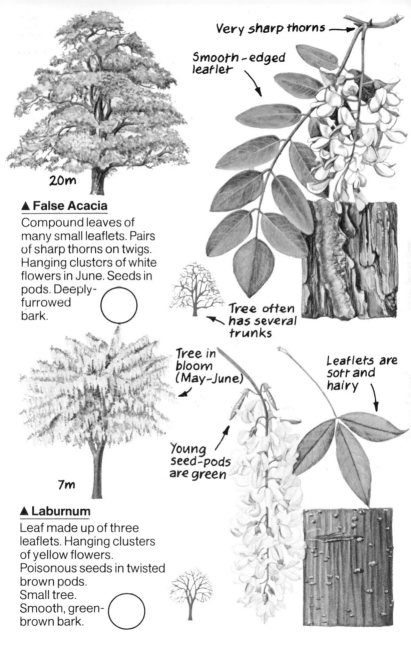

Very sharp thorns

Smooth-edged leaflet

▲ False Acacia

Compound leaves of many small leaflets. Pairs of sharp thorns on twigs. Hanging clusters of white flowers in June. Seeds in pods. Deeply-furrowed bark.

20m

Tree often has several trunks

Tree in bloom (May-June)

Leaflets are soft and hairy

Young seed-pods are green

▲ Laburnum

Leaf made up of three leaflets. Hanging clusters of yellow flowers. Poisonous seeds in twisted brown pods. Small tree. Smooth, green-brown bark.

7m

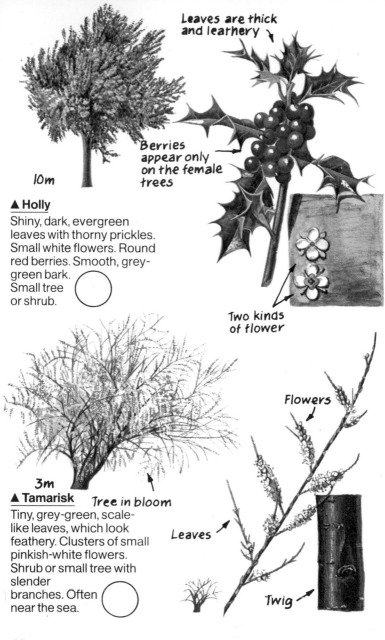

Leaves are thick and leathery

Berries appear only on the female trees

▲ Holly

Shiny, dark, evergreen leaves with thorny prickles. Small white flowers. Round red berries. Smooth, grey-green bark. Small tree or shrub.

Two kinds of flower

Tree in bloom

Flowers

Leaves

Twig

3m

▲ Tamarisk

Tiny, grey-green, scale-like leaves, which look feathery. Clusters of small pinkish-white flowers. Shrub or small tree with slender branches. Often near the sea.

46

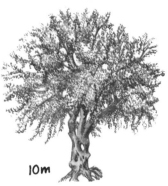

10m

▲ Common Olive

Narrow evergreen leaves
in pairs. Clusters of small
whitish flowers. Fleshy
green fruit ripens
to black. Small tree
with twisted trunk.

Edible fruits
are oily with
hard stones

(Not in
Britain)

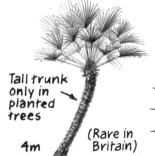

Tall trunk
only in
planted
trees

4m

(Rare in
Britain)

▲ European Fan Palm

Large, fan-shaped leaves
made up of 12-15 stiff,
pointed parts. Large
clusters of small flowers
and fruits. Wild
plants form
trunkless clumps
of leaves.

Hairy
trunk

47

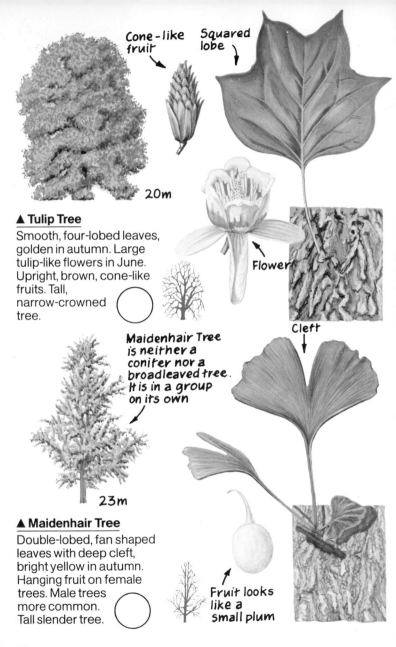

Cone-like fruit

Squared lobe

20m

Flower

Cleft

▲ Tulip Tree

Smooth, four-lobed leaves, golden in autumn. Large tulip-like flowers in June. Upright, brown, cone-like fruits. Tall, narrow-crowned tree.

Maidenhair Tree is neither a conifer nor a broadleaved tree. It is in a group on its own

23m

▲ Maidenhair Tree

Double-lobed, fan shaped leaves with deep cleft, bright yellow in autumn. Hanging fruit on female trees. Male trees more common. Tall slender tree.

Fruit looks like a small plum

Shrubs

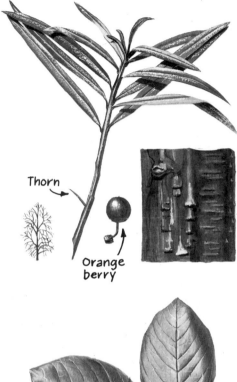

▲ Sea Buckthorn

Long, narrow, greyish-green leaves. Thorny twigs. Tiny, green flowers. Orange berries. Grows in dense thickets mainly by the sea.

2m

Thorn

Orange berry

▲ Alder Buckthorn

Dull green, oval leaves, turning yellow in autumn. Small greenish flowers. Red berries turn black when ripe. Small tree or shrub. Damp places.

4m

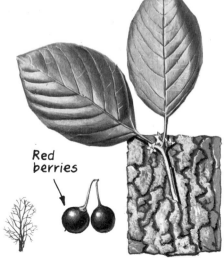

Red berries

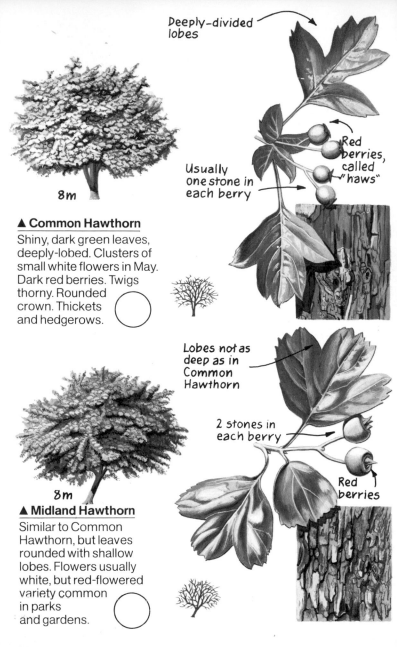

Deeply-divided lobes

Red berries, called "haws"

Usually one stone in each berry

▲ Common Hawthorn

Shiny, dark green leaves, deeply-lobed. Clusters of small white flowers in May. Dark red berries. Twigs thorny. Rounded crown. Thickets and hedgerows.

8m

Lobes not as deep as in Common Hawthorn

2 stones in each berry

Red berries

▲ Midland Hawthorn

Similar to Common Hawthorn, but leaves rounded with shallow lobes. Flowers usually white, but red-flowered variety common in parks and gardens.

8m

3 lobes

Red berries

Large outer flowers

Tiny inner flowers

3m

▲ Guelder Rose

Leaves with 3-5 toothed lobes, turning russet in autumn. Clusters of white flowers, inner flowers much smaller. Red berries. Hedgerow shrub.

12m

Lowest pair of lobes are the most deeply divided

Dark grey bark becomes furrowed with age

▲ Wild Service Tree

Leaves five-lobed, turning deep red in autumn. Clusters of white flowers in May. Drab brown, speckled berries. Small rounded tree.

Flower

Identifying Winter Buds

In winter you can identify broad-leaved trees by their winter buds.

English Oak
Clusters of stout, light brown buds on rugged twigs.

Turkey Oak
Clusters of small, brown, whiskered buds.

Red Oak
Clusters of reddish-brown buds on grey-green twigs with large bud at the tip.

Ash
Large black buds on silver-grey twigs.

Alder
Stalked violet buds. Male catkins often present.

Rowan
Large blackish end bud with tuft of white hairs.

White Poplar
Small, orange-brown bud covered by white felty hairs on green twigs.

White Willow
Slender buds enclosed in a single scale, close to pinkish downy twig.

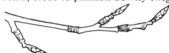

Common Beech
Long pointed, copper-brown buds sticking out from brown twigs.

Hornbeam
Dull brown or green buds, close to fine, greyish-brown twigs.

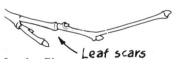

London Plane
Brown, cone-shaped buds with ring scars round them.

Sycamore
Large green buds with dark-edged scales on stout, light brown twigs.

English Elm
Pointed, hairy, chocolate-brown buds on stout twigs.

Leaf scars

Common Walnut
Big, black, velvety, triangle-shaped buds on stout, hollow twigs.

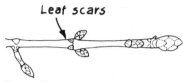

Leaf scars

Horse Chestnut
Large, sticky, brown buds on stout twigs, with obvious leaf scars.

False Acacia
Small buds with thorns at base on grey, crooked, ribbed twigs.

Wild Service Tree
Flat, green buds with brown-edged scales on thick, light-brown twigs.

Sweet Chestnut
Rounded, reddish-brown buds on knobbly, greenish-brown twigs.

Wild Cherry
Fat, shiny, red-brown buds grouped at tip of light brown twigs.

Leaf scars

Tulip Tree
Flat, purplish buds with short stalk on light brown twigs.

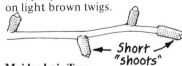

← Short "shoots" →

Maidenhair Tree
Squat, reddish-brown buds on fawn-coloured twigs.

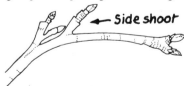

← Side shoot

Crab Apple
Small, hairy, brown, triangle-shaped buds, often bent to one side, on shiny twigs.

Common Lime
Reddish-brown, lop-sided buds on reddish twigs.

Bark Quiz

Name the trees these bark rubbings are from. The answers are upside-down at the bottom of the page.

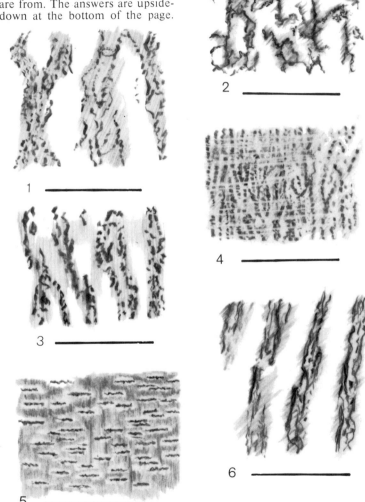

1

2

3

4

5

6

1. Walnut 2. London Plane 3. English Oak 4. Common Beech 5. Silver Birch 6. Sweet Chestnut 7. Scots Pine 8. Whitebeam 9. Lombardy Poplar 10. Larch.

54

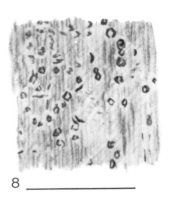

7 _____

8 _____

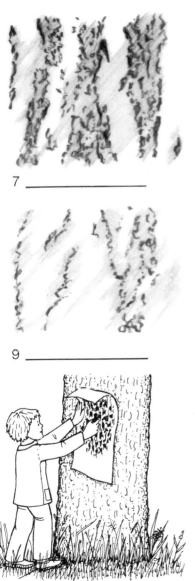

9 _____

10 ____

Making Bark Rubbings

To make bark rubbings, you need strong thin paper, wax crayons and sellotape. Tape a piece of paper against the trunk of a tree. Rub firmly up and down on the paper with the crayon until the bark pattern appears. Be careful not to tear the paper when rubbing.

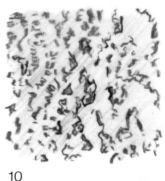

Match the Fruits to the Trees

Match the numbered fruits to the trees on which they grow. The answers are upside-down at the bottom of the opposite page.

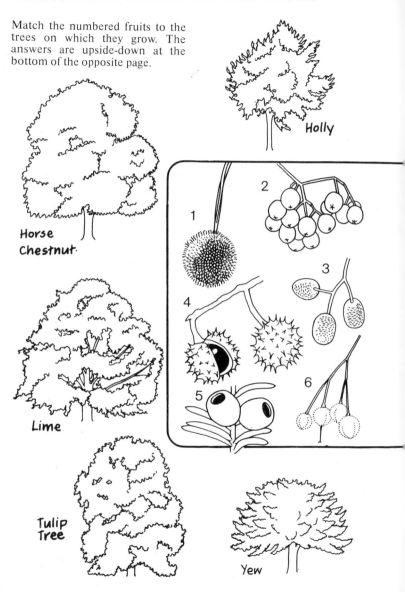

Holly

Horse Chestnut

Lime

Tulip Tree

Yew

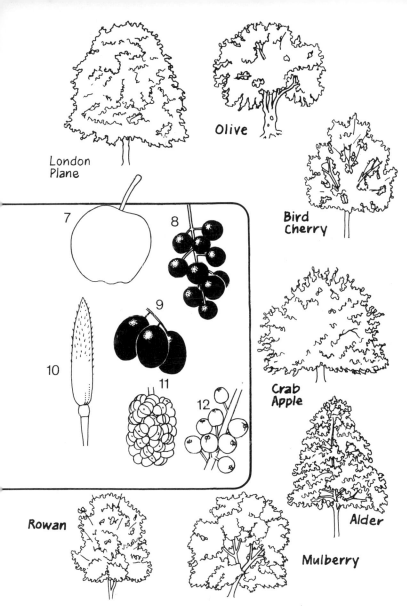

London Plane

Olive

Bird Cherry

Crab Apple

Alder

Mulberry

Rowan

7

8

9

10

11

12

1. London Plane 2. Rowan 3. Alder 4. Horse Chestnut 5. Yew 6. Lime 7. Crab Apple 8. Bird Cherry 9. Olive 10. Tulip Tree 11. Black Mulberry 12. Holly

57

Growing Seedlings

Try growing your own tree from a seed. Pick ripe seeds from trees or from the ground. Acorns are especially easy to find and grow, but almost any fresh seed will do. Most seeds take a couple of months to sprout.

1

Soak the acorns or other hard nuts overnight in warm water. Take the cups off the acorns, but do not try to remove their shells.

2

Put some stones or pebbles in the bottom of a flower pot. This will help the water to drain properly. Fill the pot with soil or compost until the pot is almost full. Place a saucer under the pot and water the soil well.

3

Because the seeds need plenty of room to grow, place only one seed in each pot that you have prepared. Cover the seed with a thin layer of soil. Press the soil down to make it firm. Water the soil again lightly.

4
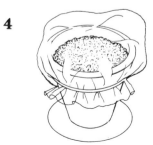

Place a plastic bag over the top of each pot and fasten it with string or a rubber band. This will help to keep the soil inside the pot moist without any watering. Place the pot on a window-sill if possible, or in a sunny place. Wait for the seeds to sprout.

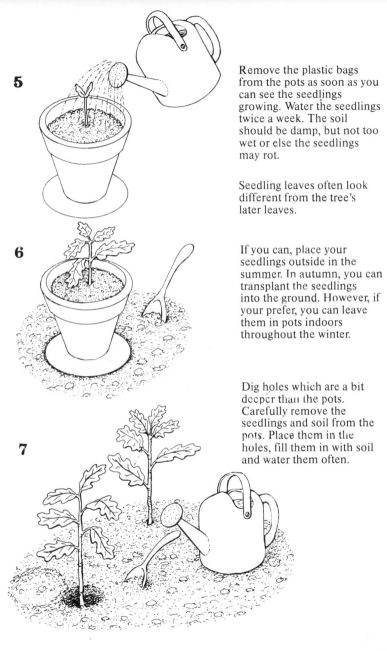

5 Remove the plastic bags from the pots as soon as you can see the seedlings growing. Water the seedlings twice a week. The soil should be damp, but not too wet or else the seedlings may rot.

Seedling leaves often look different from the tree's later leaves.

6 If you can, place your seedlings outside in the summer. In autumn, you can transplant the seedlings into the ground. However, if your prefer, you can leave them in pots indoors throughout the winter.

Dig holes which are a bit deeper than the pots. Carefully remove the seedlings and soil from the pots. Place them in the holes, fill them in with soil and water them often.

7

Books to Read

For identification: *Know Your Broadleaves* and *Know Your Conifers*. H. L. Edlin (H.M.S.O.). Two paperbacks from the Forestry Commission. Good value.
Trees in Britain. (Jarrold). A series of five cheap booklets, with colour photographs.
A Field Guide to the Trees of Britain and Northern Europe. A. Mitchell (Collins). Good, detailed reference book to carry round.
Trees of the world. S. Leathart (Hamlyn).
Large book with colour photographs. Worth getting out of the library.
Trees and Bushes of Europe. O. Polunin (Oxford). Lots of colour photographs.
For reading: *The NatureTrail Book of Trees & Leaves.* I. Selberg (Usborne). Facts about trees and how they grow. Lots of projects, eg. making a tree survey and making leaf tiles. Good value.
The World of a Tree. A. Darlington (Faber). All about the animals and insects that live in and around trees.
Town & Country: Growing Trees. I. Finch (Longman). How trees grow. Cheap paperback.

Places to Visit

These are gardens open to the public and are very good places to spot trees.
Royal Botanic Gardens, Kew, Richmond, Surrey.
Regent's Park, London.
Hyde Park, London.
Royal Horticultural Society Gardens, Wisley, Ripley, Surrey.
Borde Hill, Haywards Heath, Sussex.
Royal Botanic Gardens, Wakehurst Place, Ardingly, nr. Haywards Heath, Surrey.
Sheffield Park, Uckfield, Sussex.
Winkworth Arboretum, Godalming, Surrey.
Syon House, Brentford, Middx.
Cambridge University Botanic Gardens, Cambridge.
Oxford University Botanic Gardens, Oxford.
The National Pinetum, Bedgebury, Goudhurst, Kent.
Savill Gardens, Windsor, Berks.
Bolderwood Arboretum, New Forest, Hants.
Exebury, Beaulieu, Hants.
Eastnor Castle, Ledbury, Herefordshire.
Stourhead, Mere, Wilts.
Westonbirt Arboretum, nr. Tetbury, Glos.
Speech House, Coleford, Glos.
Bath Botanic Gardens, Bath, Avon.
Bicton Gardens, East Budleigh, Devon.
Liverpool University Botanic Gardens, Liverpool.
Chatsworth House, Derbyshire.
Harlow Car Gardens, Harrogate, Yorks.
Bodnant Gardens, Tal-y-cefn, Conway, Clwyd.
Vivod Forest Garden, Llangollen, Clwyd.
Royal Botanic Gardens, Edinburgh.
Inverary Castle, Argyllshire.
Younger Botanic Gardens, Benmore, by Dunoon, Argyllshire.
Diana's Grove, Blair Castle, Blair Atholl, Perthshire.

Latin Names

Here is a list of the names of the trees in this book, in Latin. The common (English) name may vary from one part of the country to another, but the Latin name remains the same.

Index